My Guide to the
CONSTITUTION

THE
JUDICIAL
BRANCH

Pete DiPrimio

Mitchell Lane
PUBLISHERS

P.O. Box 196
Hockessin, Delaware 19707

My Guide to the CONSTITUTION

THE BILL OF RIGHTS
THE EXECUTIVE BRANCH
THE JUDICIAL BRANCH
THE LEGISLATIVE BRANCH
THE POWER OF THE STATES
THE STORY OF THE CONSTITUTION

PUBLISHER'S NOTE: The Constitution of the United States appears in the appendix to My Guide to the Constitution: *The Story of the Constitution*. The amendments to the Constitution, including the Bill of Rights, appear in the appendix to My Guide to the Constitution: *The Bill of Rights*.

    The facts on which this book is based have been thoroughly researched. Documentation of such research can be found on page 44. While every possible effort has been made to ensure accuracy, the publisher will not assume liability for damages caused by inaccuracies in the data, and makes no warranty on the accuracy of the information contained herein.

AUTHOR'S NOTE: This story is retold using dialogue as an aid to readability. The dialogue is based on the author's research, which is detailed on page 44.

Printing 1 2 3 4 5 6 7 8 9

Library of Congress
Cataloging-in-Publication Data
DiPrimio, Pete.
  The judicial branch / by Pete DiPrimio.
    p. cm. —(My guide to the Constitution)
  Includes bibliographical references and index.
  ISBN 978-1-58415-944-5 (library bound)
  1. United States. Supreme Court—Juvenile literature. 2. Courts of last resort—United States—Juvenile literature. I. Title.
  KF8742.D57 2011
  347.73'26—dc22

                         2011002753

Paperback ISBN: 9781612281865
eBook ISBN: 9781612280882

                                    PLB

CONTENTS

Words in bold type can be found in the glossary.

Chapter 1

How the Supreme Court Became the Supreme Court

James Madison roasted in the stifling heat of a brutal Philadelphia summer night. Closed windows robbed the State House of even a breeze. Three candles cast flickering shadows across the empty meeting room. Madison swatted at a swarm of bluebottle flies in a battle he couldn't win—much like the contest of wills he faced with the other delegates in this Constitutional Convention that threatened to never end.

It was 1787 and this thirty-six-year-old Virginia politician couldn't stop worrying. The United States, a country he had done so much to help create a few years earlier, was in big trouble. Defeating the British, the most powerful nation on earth, in the **Revolutionary War** was easy compared to running a country.

Loud footsteps thudded against the wooden floor. A tall figure loomed by the doorway.

"Get some sleep," George Washington said. "It will be better in the morning. It's always better in the morning." He flashed a weary and rare smile. "It can't be any worse."

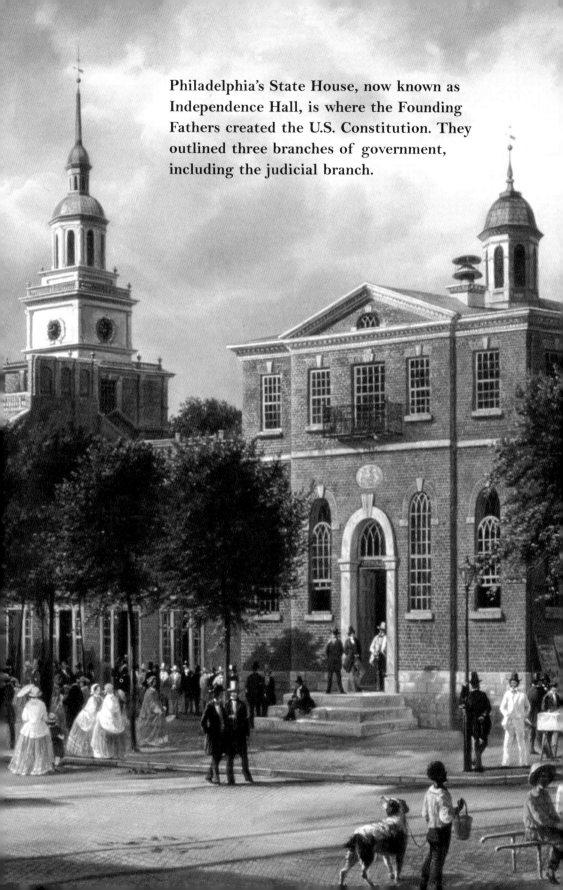

Philadelphia's State House, now known as Independence Hall, is where the Founding Fathers created the U.S. Constitution. They outlined three branches of government, including the judicial branch.

James Madison, 1792

Madison waved good night. Washington was the official president of the convention that was designed to fix things, but Madison ran the show. Badly, it seemed, if you believed critics such as Patrick Henry.

The national government was originally based on the Articles of Confederation, and it was a mess. It wasn't a government as much as a "friendship" between thirteen states that acted like separate countries. People were, say, Virginians or New Yorkers first, and then Americans. The central government had little power. It couldn't tax its citizens, set trade policy with other countries, or settle disputes between states. It couldn't even raise money to wage war.

Madison and the other delegates had gathered to write a new **constitution** that would create a government the world had never seen before. It would include a judicial branch, an executive branch, and a legislative branch. After months of meetings and debates, the new Constitution was read and signed on September 17, 1787, and **ratified** on June 21, 1788.

Once the Constitution was ratified, there was still a lot of work to do, especially with the judicial branch, which would include a Supreme Court and lower (or "inferior") courts. How would it be organized? How powerful would it be?

Answers started coming from the First Congress. It began on September 24, 1789, with a bill by Connecticut Senator Oliver Ellsworth. He had been a deputy at the Constitutional Convention. He would later become chief justice of the Supreme Court, but at this time, he was just trying to make sense of what powers the Supreme Court would have.

The Constitution is vague about the Supreme Court. It leaves its makeup and the creation of lower courts up to Congress. Here's what it says, in Article III, sections 1 and 2:

Section 1. The judicial power of the United States shall be vested in one Supreme Court and in such inferior courts that the Congress may from time to time ordain and establish.

Section 2. The judicial power shall extend to all cases, in law and equity, arising under the Constitution, the laws of the United States and Treaties.

That is basically all Ellsworth had to work with, and he made the best of it. His bill organized the Supreme Court with a chief justice (the judge in charge) and five associate justices. Each state would have a district court, for a total of 13 district courts. The bill also created three circuit courts of appeal. Running them would be clerks, marshals, and district attorneys. (There are now 12 circuit courts of appeal, including one for Washington, D.C., and 94 district courts.)

So what are the roles of all these courts?

District courts are courts of original jurisdiction. That means they are the local trial courts in the federal system. Most decisions in these courts are final, but if a person wants to appeal because he or she does not agree with the decision, the case can be brought before a court of appeal. Courts of appeal are organized into circuits (which cover large areas of the country). When they were organized in 1789, they were called circuits because they would move slowly in "circuits" from town to town to serve the far-flung population.

If the decision from the court of appeal is still unsatisfactory, the case may be brought before the U.S. Supreme Court—the final court of appeal. It can hear cases from federal courts and from state courts when a federal issue is involved. Federal issues include crimes against the United States, disputes among citizens of different states, disputes between U.S. citizens and those of another country, and decisions affecting the Constitution.

The Ellsworth Bill also created a brand-new position, the Attorney General, who is basically the main legal adviser for the president. The role has since expanded, and the position is part of the president's cabinet (so the Attorney General is appointed by the president). The Attorney General now runs the Department of Justice and is considered the government's top lawyer and law enforcement officer. States also

Eric Holder (left) became Attorney General under President Barack Obama.

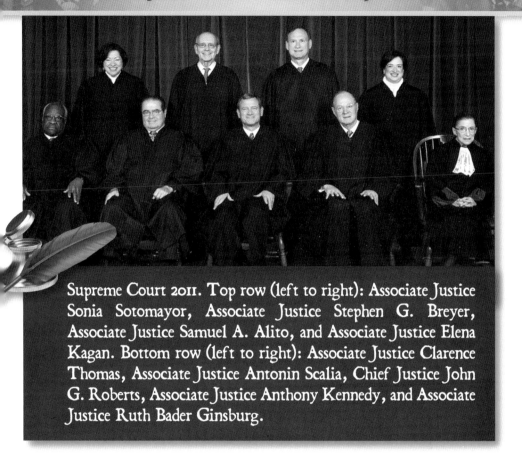

Supreme Court 2011. Top row (left to right): Associate Justice Sonia Sotomayor, Associate Justice Stephen G. Breyer, Associate Justice Samuel A. Alito, and Associate Justice Elena Kagan. Bottom row (left to right): Associate Justice Clarence Thomas, Associate Justice Antonin Scalia, Chief Justice John G. Roberts, Associate Justice Anthony Kennedy, and Associate Justice Ruth Bader Ginsburg.

have attorneys general, and those are usually chosen by popular elections. When it was passed, the Ellsworth Bill became known as the Judiciary Act of 1789, or Ellsworth Act.

The U.S. Supreme Court is officially known as the Supreme Court of the United States. Members are addressed as "Justice" or "Associate Justice." The head of the court is always the Chief Justice of the United States and is specifically mentioned in the Constitution (Article I, section 3).

Another act, passed on February 24, 1807, boosted the number of associate justices to six. In March 1837, there were eight associate justices. In March 1863, another associate justice was added to make it nine.

In 1866, Congress passed a law that said no more associate justices could be appointed until the number dropped back to six. The law was changed again in 1869 to get the number back to eight associate justices. That is where it remains.

Sometimes people get confused and think that the Supreme Court can directly nullify, or cancel out, an act of Congress. The Court does not have that power. What it can do is examine a law when a suit is brought before it. If the Court rules that the law follows the Constitution, it is allowed to stay. If the Court rules that the law goes beyond the powers granted by the Constitution, then it either has to be rewritten or it becomes ineffective.

The Constitution also gives the Supreme Court the power to determine if someone commits **treason** against the United States. A treasonous act is one that can harm the country, such as by declaring war against the United States or by aiding America's enemies. To be convicted, there have to

In 1859, John Brown and some of his sons snuck into a Virginia military base to steal weapons for a rebellion. He was captured, convicted of treason, and sentenced to death by hanging.

be two witnesses to the treason or an open confession in court. Congress has the power to determine punishment, which can include death.

The Supreme Court also rules on something called "reasonable construction" of the Constitution. The U.S. government has only the powers specifically granted to it by the Constitution (called limited powers), yet it is constantly passing laws and exercising powers that are not mentioned in the Constitution. "Reasonable construction" makes that possible. For example, the Constitution gives the government the right to make money. "Reasonable construction" allows the government to design the money (such as by putting George Washington's face on one-dollar bills and determining the type of paper used).

In some states, the court of appeal may be called the state supreme court. District court, circuit court, superior court, and court of common pleas are also all at the same level in the judicial system.

Chapter 2

Not Backing Down

John and Mary Beth Tinker weren't about to back down, not from the principal or anyone else. They were high school students in Des Moines, Iowa, and in the late 1960s they believed that the war in Vietnam was wrong. To show people how they felt, they went to school wearing black armbands.

School officials thought the display was unpatriotic and had no place in school. They told the Tinkers to take off the armbands. When the Tinkers refused, they were suspended.

The Tinkers and their parents didn't think that was right. They insisted the students had the right of free speech based on the Constitution's First Amendment. They sued the school, and the case went all the way to the Supreme Court.

The Supreme Court ruled that the Tinkers had the right to wear the armbands and the school was wrong to suspend them. Justice Abe Fortas said that no one expects students to "shed their constitutional rights to freedom of speech or expression at the schoolhouse gate."

Vietnam War protesters had the right to peacefully gather outside the entrance to the Pentagon on October 21, 1967. Military police were there to keep them out of the Pentagon.

John and Mary Beth Tinker show the black armbands (that included the white peace symbol) banned by their Des Moines, Iowa, school system. The Supreme Court ruled those armbands could not be banned because of the Tinkers' right to free speech.

By reviewing whether an act is Constitutional or not, the Supreme Court can affect the lives of people all over the United States.

There are other famous cases. For example, a lot of schools used to be separated by race, which is called **segregation**. Black students could not go to schools for whites.

All that changed after Linda Brown and her family sued their local school board. Linda lived in Topeka, Kansas, in the early 1950s and went to an all-black elementary school. She and her sister had to walk through a dangerous railroad yard to get to the bus stop for the ride to school. There was a school closer to their house, but it was for white students only. Linda and her family felt they had the right to go to the white school. The Fourteenth Amendment, passed in 1866, abolished slavery and declared that all citizens were due equal protection of the law. The family said segregation violated the Fourteenth Amendment. Federal district court ruled that segregation in public education put black children at a disadvantage, but because all-black schools and all-white schools had similar buildings, transportation, classes, and teachers, it was legal. This ruling was nicknamed "separate but equal."

The Browns appealed to the U.S. Supreme Court. They said similar schools could never be equal. The Court agreed in its 1954 decision. It said state laws requiring separate but equal schools violated the equal protection clause of the Fourteenth Amendment.

Remember, the Supreme Court decides whether or not a law—such as segregating schools between whites and blacks—is constitutional. If it is, the law stays. If it is not, the law is tossed out. That is true of both state and federal laws. If the president pushes for a law, and Congress debates and passes it, the Supreme Court can still declare it **unconstitutional**, and the law will be removed.

Federal judges are not elected to terms. The time they serve does not expire. This protects them from voters who are angry with their decisions and lets them decide the law with only justice in mind. All Supreme Court justices are nominated by the president and confirmed by the Senate. They may retire, however; and they can be **impeached** (removed from office by Congress).

The Supreme Court has to have full independence. Judges cannot be fired or punished for making unpopular judgments. Also, to make sure Justices aren't bribed, the Constitution states they should get a salary that cannot be decreased while they are in office. In 2010, the Chief Justice made $223,500 a year. Associate justices made $213,900 a year.

The president can nominate anyone he or she wants, and the Senate usually confirms the president's choice. By 2010, of the 132 people nominated for justice, 27 were rejected. While the Founding Fathers wanted to keep politics out of the Supreme Court, not every president has done so. In 1987, the Senate rejected President Ronald Reagan's choice, Robert Bork, because it thought he was too conservative.

Sometimes the confirmation hearings can get intense. In 2009, after heavy debate, the Senate voted 68–31 to confirm President Barack

Obama's choice of Sonia Sotomayor. Obama praised the vote, saying, "With this historic vote, the Senate has affirmed that Justice Sotomayor has the intellect, the temperament, the history, the integrity and the independence of mind to ably serve on our highest court."

Here is some information on the nine Supreme Court justices who were in office in 2011:

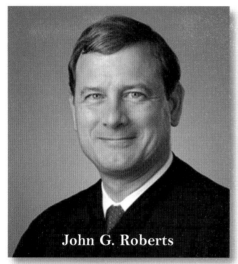

John G. Roberts

Chief Justice **John G. Roberts** was born in 1955. After graduating from Harvard Law School in 1979, he was a Supreme Court law clerk. He also worked in the U.S. Department of Justice, in the White House under President Ronald Reagan, and practiced law in Washington, D.C., for ten years. In 2003, he became a court of appeal judge. When Sandra Day O'Connor retired in 2005, President George W. Bush nominated Roberts as Chief Justice of the Supreme Court, and he took the bench on September 29 of that year. Known for being conservative on the bench, he asks quick, sharp questions in court.

Samuel Alito was born in 1950. After graduating from Yale Law School in 1975, he was an assistant U.S. attorney in New Jersey, worked for the Department of Justice, and was appointed to the court of appeal. President George W. Bush nominated him to the Supreme

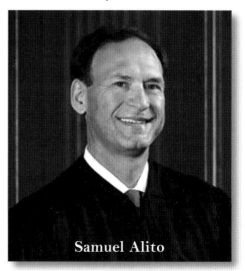

Samuel Alito

Court, and he took the bench on January 31, 2006. Alito is considered to be very serious and persistent. He asks questions that narrow down the choices for how a ruling will turn out.

Antonin Scalia was born in 1936. Another Harvard Law School graduate, he had a private practice in

Antonin Scalia

Ohio; was a law professor at the University of Virginia, Georgetown University, and Stanford University; and then was a judge for a court of appeal. President Ronald Reagan nominated him as associate justice, and he started on September 26, 1986. He is considered brash, wisecracking, fast-talking, and extremely conservative politically. Privately, he likes to go duck hunting.

Stephen Breyer

Stephen Breyer was born in 1938. After graduating from Harvard Law School, he worked as a Supreme Court law clerk for the U.S. Attorney General, and as an assistant prosecutor for the Watergate case against President Richard Nixon. Later, he was a law professor at Harvard, the College of Law in Australia, and the University of Rome, and he also served as a court of appeal judge. President Bill Clinton nominated him for the Supreme Court, and he started on

July 29, 1994. He is known for using **hypothetical** questions to make decisions.

Ruth Bader Ginsburg was born in 1933 and graduated from Columbia Law School. She was a law professor at Rutgers and Columbia, and then a court of appeal judge. Known for being politically correct, she was a leader of the women's movement in the 1970s and continues to promote women's rights. President Bill Clinton nominated her for the court, and she started on August 3, 1993. Even-tempered and quiet, she reportedly loves music and opera, and is a stickler for avoiding misstatements and misapplied facts.

Ruth Bader Ginsburg

Elena Kagan was born in 1960 and also graduated from Harvard Law School. She was a law clerk for the Supreme Court; an attorney in Washington, D.C.; a law professor at the University of Chicago and Harvard; and an associate counsel for President Bill Clinton. She became the dean of Harvard Law School in 2003, and then the **Solicitor General** of the United States. President Barrack Obama nominated her, and she started on August 7, 2010. She is the only member of the Supreme Court who lacks past experience as a judge.

Elena Kagan

Anthony Kennedy

Anthony Kennedy was born in 1936 and graduated from Harvard Law School. He was in private practice in California, then a law professor at the University of the Pacific. He was a member of the California Army National Guard and on the board of the Federal Judicial Center. In 1975, he became a judge in a court of appeal. President Ronald Reagan nominated him, and he started on February 18, 1988. Kennedy is careful not to show what he's thinking or feeling in court. His questions are straightforward, and he often casts the deciding vote.

Sonia Sotomayor

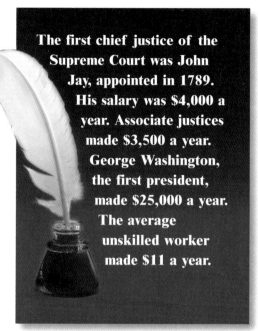

The first chief justice of the Supreme Court was John Jay, appointed in 1789. His salary was $4,000 a year. Associate justices made $3,500 a year. George Washington, the first president, made $25,000 a year. The average unskilled worker made $11 a year.

Sonia Sotomayor was born in 1954 and graduated from Yale Law School. She was an assistant district attorney in New York, a partner in a New York law firm, a district court judge, and a judge in a court of appeal. President Barack Obama nominated her, and she started on May 26, 2009. She is known as a fearless judge who cares about her family, community, and the people she serves in court. Quick and demanding with her questions, she is considered tough but fair in her decisions.

Clarence Thomas was born in 1948 and also graduated from Yale Law School. He was an assistant attorney general in Missouri, an assistant secretary for civil rights in the Department of Education, and a judge in a court of appeal. President George H. W. Bush nominated him, and he started on October 23, 1991. By 2011, he had not questioned a single lawyer in five years. Some people criticized him for this. However, he says he often remains silent because he believes lawyers should be able to make their cases without interruption.

Clarence Thomas

Chapter 3

Can the Supreme Court Pick the President?

Nobody knew what to do. The 2000 presidential election had ended in a virtual draw between Democratic candidate Al Gore, who was vice president under Bill Clinton, and Republican candidate George W. Bush, the governor of Texas. At the end of the day, the votes were very close—too close to call. Democrats declared Gore the winner. Republicans said it was Bush.

Although U.S. citizens vote in the "popular vote" for the president, an indirect election by the **Electoral College** determines the presidency. According to Article II, section 1 of the Constitution, members of the Electoral College, called electors, are chosen by each state. The number of electors equals the number of senators and representatives the state has in Congress. Usually, if a candidate wins the popular vote in a state, he or she will receive all the Electoral College votes from that state. In 2000, there were 538 electors, and a candidate needed 270 votes from the Electoral College to win the presidency.

Media, voters, and police gathered at one of the Florida recount sites in 2000. The presidential election of that year came down to a recount of the votes to decide whether Al Gore or George Bush would be president.

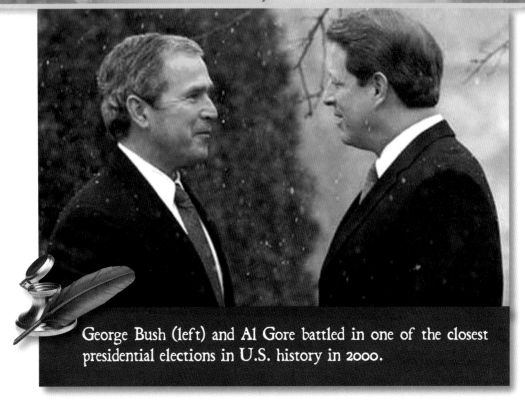

George Bush (left) and Al Gore battled in one of the closest presidential elections in U.S. history in 2000.

People went to bed on election night in November 2000 thinking Gore had won. They woke up to see that Bush had been declared the winner.

The results were so close, however, that the outcome was not official. After a lot of confusion, the election would come down to the votes from one state—Florida, which carried 25 electoral votes.

When Florida's vote was official, Bush was declared the winner. He had 271 electoral votes and Gore had 266 (one elector, from Washington, D.C., did not vote). Gore and his associates said there were votes in Florida's popular election that hadn't been counted, and there were enough of them to change who the winner was. In some districts, voters were to punch a hole in a paper **ballot**. When a ballot hadn't been properly punched through, a chad was left hanging—and these caused improper counting.

Many people, including Gore, wanted a manual recount of Florida's ballots, but Gore and Bush could not agree on how it should be done.

Both sides claimed the other party had cheated (by scaring voters, stuffing ballot boxes, and using other tactics). They sued each other at the state and federal level. The cases became known as *Bush v. Gore*. The election became so chaotic, the Supreme Court decided to step in.

Was it the right thing to do?

The U.S. Constitution divides the government into three branches—the executive (the president), the legislative (Congress), and the judicial (Supreme Court). Each branch is designed to balance the others so that no one person or group has more power than the others. The Founding Fathers wanted to make sure that a king or dictator never took charge of the country. They also wanted to make sure the country adhered to the **Rule of Law**, which has several parts:

1) All people have to obey the law of the land and shall be treated equally.
2) The government has to obey the law.
3) No one is above the law.
4) Everybody will be treated the same by the law.
5) The United States will have a "government of laws and not of men." In other words, it cannot have a king, dictator, or other sort of tyranny.

The Founding Fathers also wanted to keep Supreme Court justices out of the political process. Justices are supposed to make decisions based on the law, not on a political party or belief. Further, the Constitution promises certain rights to the states. If Florida voted to have a recount, could the Supreme Court overturn the state's decision?

The Florida Supreme Court declared that the recount in Palm Beach County could take as long as was necessary, even past the state's December 1 deadline for certifying votes. A week later the Florida Supreme Court ordered, by a 4-3 decision, a statewide recount. Every ballot in the entire state would be recounted. Officials began to check the ballots, including those that were not filled out properly or that had hanging chads. They looked at each of these to determine whether the ballot would count. They sometimes needed magnifying glasses to tell which way a vote had been cast.

The Bush side filed a request four different times in lower federal courts to stop the recount. Because Bush had apparently won, it was in his best interest not to have a recount. The lower federal courts rejected the Bush request each time.

Concerned that the chaos and confusion were hurting the country, the U.S. Supreme Court delayed the recount. Florida would have to wait until the Supreme Court decided the matter.

A few days later, in a 5-4 vote, the Supreme Court permanently stopped the Florida recount. It said the recount violated the Equal Protection Clause in section 1 of the Fourteenth Amendment: "No State shall . . . deny to any person within its jurisdiction the equal protection of the laws." In other words, the Supreme Court said the recount denied the people of Florida in general and George Bush in particular equal protection, because exceptions were being made to election rules. It overturned the state court's election laws and its ruling by using a legal theory that had never been used before. The first results would stand. Bush was officially declared the winner in Florida, and he became the 43rd President of the United States.

The decision angered a lot of people. Some pointed out that the five justices who voted to stop the recount had been nominated by Republican presidents and probably favored Bush. They said the fact that it was not a 9-0 decision suggested that it was influenced by politics and not law. Still others said that what the Supreme Court did was right and saved the country from a lot of hardship.

Afterward, recounts showed that, by using one method, Bush would have won anyway. Using another method, Gore would have won.

The Supreme Court said its decision in *Bush v. Gore* should not be used in future cases. Years later, *60 Minutes* correspondent Lesley Stahl asked Associate Justice Antonin Scalia whether the Court had made the right decision. He said people should just "get over it."

In this 1876 cartoon about the controversial presidential election between Democrat Samuel J. Tilden and Republican Rutherford B. Hayes, Tilden cries, "Boo Hoo! Ruthy Hayes's got my presidency and won't give it to me."

Only one other time has the Supreme Court influenced a presidential race. That came in 1876 when Samuel J. Tilden, the Democratic governor of New York, ran against Rutherford B. Hayes, the Republican governor of Ohio.

After the election, Tilden looked like the winner. He won the popular vote and had 184 electoral votes to Hayes's 165. There was just one problem—Tilden needed 185 electoral votes to win.

Because of disputes, there were still 20 undecided Electoral College votes from Oregon and the southern states of Louisiana, South Carolina, and Florida. Officials would have to decide how those 20 votes should be cast. The Supreme Court turned to the Twelfth Amendment of the Constitution, which says that in a contested presidential election, "The

President of the Senate shall, in the presence of the Senate and the House of Representatives, open all the certificates and the votes shall then be counted."

In 1876, the Senate was controlled by Republicans, while the House of Representatives was controlled by Democrats. Both groups set up an electoral commission to decide who would become president. The Senate chose three Republicans and two Democrats to be on the commission. The House chose three Democrats and two Republicans. That made a total of ten, evenly divided between Democrats and Republicans. Five Supreme Court justices were also on the commission. Two were Democrats. Two were Republicans. Those four justices would choose the fifth, who was supposed to be neutral. The only neutral

This scene from *Harper's Weekly* magazine from February 17, 1877, shows the battle over electoral votes in the presidential election. The title is "Counting the Electoral Vote—David Dudley Objects to the Vote of Florida."

A political cartoon from the New York *Daily Graphic*, February 26, 1877, shows Hayes prevailing in the disputed election.

justice was David Davis. He immediately resigned.

Only Republican justices remained. When Joseph Bradley was selected for the commission, there were eight Republicans to seven Democrats.

The commission voted on party lines. Hayes got all 20 undecided Electoral College votes. He beat Tilden 185-184.

The Southern states were angry. They said they would do everything they could to delay Hayes from taking the president's office. The Republicans didn't want that, so they agreed to withdraw federal

troops still in the South from the Civil War, to give the South money, and to appoint at least one Southerner to Hayes's cabinet. That solved the stalemate, although after seeing the passion from what was called the "stolen presidency," Hayes chose not to run for a second term.

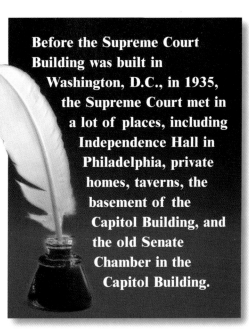

Before the Supreme Court Building was built in Washington, D.C., in 1935, the Supreme Court met in a lot of places, including Independence Hall in Philadelphia, private homes, taverns, the basement of the Capitol Building, and the old Senate Chamber in the Capitol Building.

Chapter 4

Taking Charge the John Marshall Way

John Marshall meant business. He had been a captain in the **Continental Army** during the Revolutionary War. He had lived through the brutal winter of 1777–1778 in Valley Forge and was close friends with General George Washington. He had been among the delegates who had helped shape the Constitution. He had seen four of his ten children die before they became adults.

Now he was the fourth chief justice of the Supreme Court, a man who very much believed in a strong federal government. He had a chance to show that the judicial branch could have as much power as the president and Congress. All he needed was a case, and in 1803, it came: *Marbury v. Madison.*

William Marbury didn't want much—just the job he had been appointed to fill. President John Adams picked Marbury to be the justice of the peace for the District of Columbia. But there was a problem. The commission for the job had to be delivered by the Secretary of State—John Marshall. Marshall did not

The John Marshall statue, located in John Marshall Park in the Judiciary Square neighborhood of Washington, D.C., honors one of the most influential Supreme Court Justices in U.S. history.

President John Adams (pictured) didn't realize the controversy that would follow in 1803 when he named William Marbury to be justice of the peace for the District of Columbia.

deliver it before leaving the secretary of state post, and his replacement, James Madison, refused to do so. Marbury sued, asking that the Supreme Court order Madison to deliver it.

Marshall said, in so many words, no way. He said the law that authorized the Supreme Court to do what Marbury asked was unconstitutional. This was the first example of **judicial review**—the power to determine whether an act or law is constitutional—and it was the first step in making the judicial branch the equal of the executive and the legislative branches. The decision helped to define the government's system of checks and balances.

Marshall would take other steps during his thirty-four years as chief justice (1801–1835). For instance, states didn't want to give up any of their rights. They used the Tenth Amendment, which said they had the right to govern everything in their state as long as it was not specifically assigned to the federal government by the Constitution. Then came the case of *Martin v. Hunter's Lessee* in 1816. Virginia's supreme court said that the state government and federal government were equal, and that the U.S. Supreme Court could not tell the Virginia court what to do. Wrong, Marshall said. He ruled that every state had lost some of its power when it accepted the Constitution. All states had to follow the rulings of the U.S. Supreme Court.

In the case of *McCulloch v. Maryland* in 1819, the Supreme Court ruled that Maryland could not impose a state tax on a federal bank. Marshall ruled that because the Constitution had ordered the existence of the bank, the bank had to carry out its duties. The state tax, which would have put the bank out of business, was declared unconstitutional. This established the Supreme Court's right to review state governments. Since then, the Supreme Court has used judicial review most often with state law.

Marshall and President Thomas Jefferson, a cousin, didn't agree very often. One of the most famous times came in 1807 during the trial of Aaron Burr, the former vice president under Jefferson. Burr was tried for treason. He was accused of trying to form an empire in the western part of what is now the United States. Marshall **acquitted** him (declared

Aaron Burr was the vice president of the United States under Thomas Jefferson and nearly became president, but he is most famous for killing Founding Father Alexander Hamilton in an 1804 duel.

him innocent) because the Constitution said two witnesses were needed to prove the charge, and there were not two witnesses.

Marshall was not the only great Supreme Court justice. Others such as Oliver Wendell Holmes (1902–1932) and Benjamin Cardozo (1932–1938) also had tremendous influence. One of Holmes's most famous statements was, "The life of the law has not been logic, but experience."

Because of these people, the Supreme Court continues to affect the country in big and small ways. If you've ever seen a TV show where police read a crime suspect his rights ("You have the right to remain silent; anything you say can and will be used against you in a court of law. You have the right to an attorney; if you cannot afford an attorney, one will be provided for you"), it is because of the *Miranda v. Arizona* Supreme Court decision of 1966. Ernesto Miranda was arrested after a crime victim identified him. Police questioned him without informing

Ernesto Miranda (far left) is shown with other men during his 1963 police lineup. His case led to the Supreme Court ruling that police must read suspects their rights before questioning them.

DEFENDANT	LOCATION

SPECIFIC WARNING REGARDING INTERROGATIONS

1. You have the right to remain silent.

2. Anything you say can and will be used against you in a court of law.

3. You have the right to talk to a lawyer and have him present with you while you are being questioned.

4. If you cannot afford to hire a lawyer one will be appointed to represent you before any questioning, if you wish one.

SIGNATURE OF DEFENDANT	DATE
WITNESS	TIME

☐ REFUSED SIGNATURE   SAN FRANCISCO POLICE DEPARTMENT   PR.9.1.4

Defendants are asked to sign a Miranda card carried by police.

him of his Fifth Amendment right against self-incrimination and his Sixth Amendment right to have a lawyer. While he confessed to the crime, his attorney later argued that the confession should not have been allowed in his trial. The Supreme Court agreed. It said the police should have informed Miranda of his rights. Ever since, police must read suspects their rights before questioning them.

Another important decision came in January 2010. The Supreme Court ruled, 5-4, that the government could not ban big businesses from giving a lot of money to people running for office. Businesses could give as much money as they wanted to candidates. Labor unions could do the same thing. Supporters said that because of the First Amendment right of free speech, the government could not deny this expression of support for a political candidate. Critics said the money would hurt the country. They said candidates might make laws that would help the businesses that gave them the most money. Experts said the decision would change the way elections are held.

"The people made the Constitution, and the people can unmake it. It is the creature of their will, and lives only by their will."
—Chief Justice John Marshall, 1821

Chapter 5

Supreme Power

Harry S. Truman flexed his presidential muscles in 1952 and dared somebody to stop him. He had a job to do, a country to run, and a war to win in Korea. The last thing he needed was a nationwide steel **strike**. Without steel, how could America make the equipment it needed to fight the war? When workers and management could not reach a contract agreement and the steel plants were about to be shut down, Truman ordered the army to take them over. He said he could do this as commander in chief of the military. He'd done it before with railroads and meatpackers, all in the name of national emergency. This was more of the same.

In this case, however, the Supreme Court declared the takeover was unconstitutional. Without approval from Congress, a president does not have the right to take private property.

The last thing President Richard Nixon wanted to do was to hand over what were called the Watergate tapes. Those tapes—recordings of conversations in

Realizing that he would be impeached and forced out of office, President Richard Nixon (pictured right as he leaves the White House in 1974) resigned and turned over the office to the vice president, Gerald Ford (left).

the White House during Nixon's presidency—might provide evidence of a cover-up. They might prove he was involved in the Watergate break-in of Democratic National Headquarters in 1972. Nixon said **executive power** gave him the right to refuse when investigators demanded the tapes. The Supreme Court ordered Nixon to turn over the tapes. It ruled that he did not have absolute executive power and did not have "unqualified presidential immunity" from the legal process. The tapes revealed that Nixon knew about the cover-up. Before Congress could impeach him, Nixon resigned. He was the first and only president to do so.

Franklin Delano Roosevelt was fed up with the Supreme Court. It was 1937 and he was trying to get the country out of the Great Depression. His New Deal was designed to do that, but the Supreme Court kept getting in the way. It had declared eight of his laws unconstitutional, even though Roosevelt was a very popular president and his New Deal programs were widely supported. Roosevelt tried to put five more justices on the Court who liked his ideas, making a total

The Supreme Court did not stop President Franklin Delano Roosevelt from signing the Social Security Act into law in 1935 as part of his New Deal legislation.

of fourteen justices instead of nine. The plan was for the new justices to vote in Roosevelt's favor and prevent the Supreme Court from interfering. Congress refused to let him do it. The Supreme Court could continue using judicial review to study all aspects of government, including the New Deal. If the court ruled that the policies were unconstitutional, Roosevelt would have to accept the decision.

These examples show the Supreme Court's power and its role in checking and balancing the rest of government. It is the only branch that can act as interpreter of the Constitution, deciding what the Founding Fathers meant and whether or not a law or policy is constitutional.

The funny thing is, the Constitution never gave the Supreme Court this power. The Founding Fathers wisely kept the Supreme Court description vague. They only said it was the most powerful court in the country. Why? The Founding Fathers could not know what problems would occur in the future, but they wanted the Constitution and the judicial branch to be able to adapt to changing times.

There are two ways Supreme Court justices consider cases. One is with a strict interpretation, or **strict constructionalist.** The other is by a loose interpretation, or **loose constructionalist.** Strict constructionalists believe judges should follow the principle of "original intent." That means judges may do only what they believe the Founding Fathers wanted, or intended, for the United States. Strict constructionalists believe policy making should be left to the executive and legislative branches. Staying out of the business of the other branches is called **judicial restraint.**

Loose constructionalists see the Supreme Court as a tool for making social change (such as the desegregation of schools). Using the Court this way is called judicial activism. Supporters say if politicians won't do something that's good for the country, then judges should. Critics say this takes power from Congress. Former President Ronald Reagan said when he appointed judges, "The one thing that I do seek is judges who will interpret the law and not write the law."

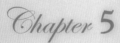

The New York Times

"All the News
That's Fit to Print"

LATE CITY EDITION

VOL. CXXII . No. 42,003   NEW YORK, TUESDAY, JANUARY 23, 1973   15 CENTS

LYNDON JOHNSON, 36TH PRESIDENT, IS DEAD; WAS ARCHITECT OF 'GREAT SOCIETY' PROGRAM

High Court Rules Abortions Legal the First 3 Months

State Bans Ruled Out Until Last 10 Weeks

National Guidelines Set by 7-to-2 Vote

By WARREN WEAVER Jr.

3.7 MILLION CARS RECALLED BY G.M. TO CORRECT FLAW

Cardinals Shocked —Reaction Mixed

By LAWRENCE VAN GELDER

KISSINGER IN PARIS; CEREMONIAL SITE CHOSEN FOR TALKS

By JERRY M. FLINT

NATION IS SHOCKED

Citizens Join Leaders in Voicing Sorrow and Paying Tribute

By ROBERT D. McFADDEN

STRICKEN AT HOME

Apparent Heart Attack Comes as Country Mourns Truman

SAN ANTONIO, Tex., Jan. 22

The nation read about the decision of *Roe v. Wade* the day former president Lyndon Johnson died, Tuesday, January 23, 1973.

One of the most controversial Supreme Court decisions involved the right to abortion. A woman in Texas wanted to have an abortion, but Texas had banned abortions. In 1973, in the case *Roe v. Wade,* the Supreme Court voted 7-2 to uphold the right of all women to have abortions, even though some states had banned them. The Court used the Fourteenth Amendment (civil rights) to support its decision.

JUDICIAL PROCESS

Article III of the Constitution guarantees that every person accused of wrongdoing has the right to a fair trial before a competent judge and a jury. The Fourth, Fifth, and Sixth Amendments (part of the Bill of Rights) provide additional protections for those accused of crimes. These include the right to a speedy trial by an impartial jury, the right to legal representation, the right to avoid self-incrimination, and protection from excessive bail, fines, and cruel and unusual punishments. Also, a person cannot be tried for the same crime twice (this is called double jeopardy).

Criminal cases are handled by either state or federal courts, depending on the kind of crime it is. There is a trial, and if a person is found guilty, a judge imposes a sentence, which can be a fine, prison time, or even death.

Civil cases deal with disputes between people or organizations. A person can sue in a civil court. A judge or a jury determines the verdict.

Decisions in criminal and civil cases can be appealed to a higher court—either to a federal court of appeal or a state court of appeal. Federal appeals are decided by panels of three judges. They get legal briefs from both sides—detailing whether there was an error and why the decision should be reversed or upheld. Then the judges rule.

People who lose in a federal court of appeal or in a state supreme court may file a petition for a **writ of certiorari**. This document asks the Supreme Court to review the lower court's decision. The Court usually hears a case only if it involves a new and important legal principle.

The Supreme Court of India in New Delhi. Protection against double jeopardy (a person's right to be tried only once for the same crime) is found in many constitutions around the world, including those of India, Canada, and Australia.

The Supreme Court gets about 7,500 requests each year. It usually chooses about 150 of them. A case is taken when four of the justices agree that it needs review.

When the Supreme Court hears a case, it studies legal briefs from the parties to the case, as well as from amicus curiae ("friends of the court"). The justices also listen to each side present its case, and then they ask questions. They hold private conferences, make their decision (which can take months), and issue an opinion that will include disagreeing arguments. At least five votes are required to make a decision.

POWER LIMITS

The Supreme Court is not all-powerful. It does not have the power to enforce its rulings. Only the executive and legislative branches of government can do that. For instance, when segregation in southern

U.S. Supreme Court,
Washington, D.C.

schools was ruled unconstitutional in 1954, nothing happened in the South at first. In 1957, when people in the South did not comply, federal troops were sent in to enforce the law.

For the most part, the Supreme Court cannot start its own cases. Cases have to come from lower courts. That way a justice can't pick a law or policy he or she disagrees with and bring it to the court for a ruling.

The Supreme Court doesn't want to interfere with the other branches, so it is rare that it totally overturns an act passed by Congress. It might overturn parts, but not the whole act. Also, it's important for politicians to obey the Supreme Court's decisions. They do so because the Constitution doesn't give them any choice.

The Supreme Court has final say in matters of law. That's the way the Founding Fathers wanted the Constitution, and government leaders are sworn to uphold it. The legacy of James Madison and John Marshall is one of the many that make the U.S. one of the strongest and fairest nations in the world.

"The most stringent protection of free speech would not protect a man in falsely shouting 'Fire!' in a theater and causing a panic."—Supreme Court Justice Oliver Wendell Holmes, 1919

"Fear of serious injury cannot alone justify suppression of free speech and assembly. Men feared witches and burned women. It is the function of speech to free men from the bondage of irrational fear." —Supreme Court Justice Louis D. Brandeis, 1927

"If the First Amendment means anything, it means that a state has no business telling a man, sitting in his own house, what books he may read or what films he may watch. Our whole constitutional heritage rebels at the thought of giving government the power to control men's minds." —Supreme Court Justice Thurgood Marshall, 1969

BOOKS

Cheney, Lynne. *A Time for Freedom: What Happened When in America.* New York: Aladdin, 2007.

Cheney, Lynne, and Greg Harlin. *We The People: The Story of Our Constitution.* New York: Simon & Schuster Children's Publishing, 2008.

McElroy, Lisa Tucker. *Sonia Sotomayor: First Hispanic U.S. Supreme Court Justice.* Minneapolis: Lerner Publishing Company, 2010.

Taylor-Butler, Christine. *The Supreme Court.* New York: Scholastic, 2008.

Travis, Cathy. *Constitution Translated for Kids / La Constitución traducida para niños.* Austin, Texas: Ovation Books, 2009.

WORKS CONSULTED

Alterman, Eric. "*Bush v. Gore's* Disgrace Deepens." *The Daily Beast,* December 4, 2010. http://www.thedailybeast.com/blogs-and-stories/2010-12-04/bush-v-gore-decision-looks-even-more-disgraceful-10-years-later/?cid=tag:all1

Biskupic, Joan. "What Are the Supreme Court Justices Really Like?" *USA Today,* March 12, 2010. http://www.usatoday.com/news/washington/judicial/supreme-court-justices-personalities.htm

CBS News. "Justice Scalia On The Record." *60 Minutes,* September 14, 2008. http://www.cbsnews.com/stories/2008/04/24/60minutes/main4040290.shtml

Ferling, John. *Setting the World Ablaze: Washington, Adams, Jefferson, and the American Revolution.* Oxford: Oxford University Press, 2000.

Higgs, Robert. "Truman's Attempt to Seize the Steel Industry." *The Freeman,* March 1, 2004. http://www.independent.org/publications/article.asp?id=1394

Lamb, Brian. *Booknotes: Stories From American History.* New York: Penguin Books, 2001.

Landmark Cases of the U.S. Supreme Court http://www.streetlaw.org/en/landmark.aspx

Levy, Leonard W. *Origins of the Bill of Rights.* New Haven, CT: Yale University Press, 2001.

Liptak, Adam. "Justices, 5-4, Reject Corporate Spending Limit." *The New York Times,* January 21, 2010.

———. "No Argument: Thomas Keeps 5-Year Silence." *The New York Times,* February 12, 2011. http://www.nytimes.com/2011/02/13/us/13thomas.html

McCullough, David. *John Adams.* New York: Simon & Schuster, 2008.

Paddock, Lisa. "Supreme Court Case Study: *Bush v. Gore.*" *Dummies.com.* http://www.dummies.com/how-to/content/supreme-court-case-study-bush-v-gore.html

Venkataraman, Nitya. "Senate Votes Sonia Sotomayor as First Hispanic Supreme Court Justice." *ABC News,* August 6, 2009.

Zack, Stephen N. "Ten Years After *Bush v. Gore,* the Court System's Independence Is under Political Attack." *The New York Daily News,* December 6, 2010. http://www.nydailynews.com/opinions/2010/12/06/2010-12-06_who_lost_bush_v_gore_courts.html

ON THE INTERNET

The Charters of Freedom: Declaration of Independence, The Constitution, The Bill of Rights
http://www.archives.gov/exhibits/charters/

Cornell University: Current U.S. Supreme Court Justices
http://www.law.cornell.edu/supct/justices/fullcourt.html

Historic Valley Forge: John Marshall
http://www.ushistory.org/valleyforge/served/marshall.html

Library of Virginia: John Marshall
http://www.lva.virginia.gov/exhibits/marshall/

U.S. Supreme Court
http://www.supremecourt.gov/

The White House: The Judicial Branch
http://www.whitehouse.gov/our-government/judicial-branch

acquit (uh-KWIT)—To clear of a charge.

ballot (BAL-it)—A paper or ticket used to cast a vote, often in an election.

constitution (kon-stih-TOO-shun)—A document that outlines the basic rules for a government.

Continental (kon-tih-NEN-tul) **Army**–The colonial army in the Revolutionary War

Electoral College (ee-LEK-tuh-rul KAH-lidj)—A group of representatives that elects the president and vice president of the United States.

executive (ek-ZEK-yoo-tiv) **power**—The power given to the president to do his job.

hypothetical (hy-poh-THEH-tih-kul)—Based on possible events rather than actual ones.

impeach (im-PEECH)—To officially accuse a public official of committing a crime.

judicial restraint (joo-DIH-shul ree-STRAYNT)—The belief that the court should hold back and let the executive and legislative branches handle policy.

judicial review (joo-DIH-shul ree-VYOO)—The Supreme Court's power to determine whether federal and state laws are constitutional.

loose constructionalist (LOOS kun-STRUK-shuh-nuh-list)—A judge who gives a wider interpretation of the law or the Constitution in order to apply it to modern society.

ratify (RAT-ih-fy)—To officially approve.

Revolutionary (reh-vuh-LOO-shuh-nayr-ee) **War**—The war between the thirteen North American colonies and Great Britain.

Rule of Law—The understanding that everyone in society, including the government, must obey the law.

segregation (seh-gruh-GAY-shun)—To separate or isolate one group from others.

Solicitor General (soh-LIH-sih-tur JEN-rul)—The senior attorney who is just below the Attorney General.

strict constructionalist (STRIKT kun-STRUK-shuh-nuh-list)—A judge who gives a narrow (strict) reading or interpretation of the Constitution.

strike—Refusal by employees to go to work in order to force their employer to agree to their demands (which often include higher pay).

treason (TREE-zun)—An act that can harm one's country, such as going to war against it or helping its enemy.

unconstitutional (un-kon-stih-TOO-shuh-nul)—Not legal under the Constitution.

writ of certiorari (RIT OF ser-shee-uh-RAYR-ee)—A file or petition from a higher court asking to review a case tried in a lower court.

ABOUT THE
AUTHOR

Pete DiPrimio is an award-winning writer and columnist for the *Fort Wayne (Indiana) News-Sentinel*, and a long-time freelance writer. He is the author of three nonfiction books pertaining to Indiana University athletics, and of *Tom Brady, Eli Manning, Drew Brees, How'd They Do That in Ancient Rome?*, and *The Sphinx* for Mitchell Lane Publishers. He graduated from Ball State University with honors, earning a Bachelor of Science degree with a minor in history. His honors thesis on the assassination of Abraham Lincoln fostered a life-long love of U.S. history and the people who shaped it. He lives in Bloomington, Indiana.